radar

cool brands

Liz Gogerly

Published in 2013 by Wayland

Copyright © Wayland 2013

Wayland
Hachette Children's Books
338 Euston Road
London NW1 3BH

Wayland Australia
Level 17/207 Kent Street
Sydney NSW 2000

Concept by Joyce Bentley

Commissioned by Debbie Foy and
Rasha Elsaeed

Produced for Wayland by Calcium
Designer: Paul Myerscough
Editor: Sarah Eason

British Library Cataloguing in Publication Data

Cool brands. — (Art on the street)(Radar)
1. Brand name products—Juvenile literature.
I. Series
741.6-dc22

ISBN: 978 0 7502 7747 1

Printed in China

Wayland is a division of Hachette Children's Books,
an Hachette UK company.

www.hachette.co.uk

Acknowledgements: Alamy: Mark Richardson 13, UK
Retail Alan King 12tr; Corbis: Cynthia Hart Designer
8, Rick Friedman 18, Sara De Boer/Retna Ltd 16-17;
Getty Images: William King cover; iStock: Brandon
Alms 26br, Skip O'Donnell 12cl, 26l, ollo 28br, Shane
Shaw 28tr, Todor Tcvetkov 3, 27, Mathias Wilson 29;
Rex: BDG 11; Shutterstock: aGinger 2r, 6-7, Galina
Barskaya 12b, BMCL 24, Eric Broder Van Dyke 9t,
clarusvisus 19, Songquan Deng 2b, 30b, ecxcn 2-3,
4-15, gary 718 1, 2t, 5, Iculig 10, Stuart Miles 31b,
Monkey Business images 31t, Tupungato 30cl; Stocks
Taylor Benson: 20-21, 21bl, 21bc, 21br.

cover stories

CONTENTS

KT-456-522

thepeople

theart

thetalk

HELLO KITTY

The cat that got the cream

THE STATS

Name: Kitty White
Born: 1 November 1974
Place of birth: Japan
Personal life: Lives with her parents, grandparents and twin sister Mimi
Job: High-flying brand!

Who's that girl?

Hello Kitty is the cute pussycat that is loved all around the world. Her face appears on everything, from pencil cases and lunchboxes to notepaper and pens. Little girls love Hello Kitty cuddly toys, while older girls are happy to sport Hello Kitty T-shirts and bags. She may look sweet, but Hello Kitty is one of the most successful brands on the planet, netting between US$1 and US$5 billion (£606 million and £3 billion) a year.

Enter the pussycat

This little ball of branding magic was created in Tokyo, Japan, in 1974 by Sanrio, a small company that produced gifts and accessories. When Sanrio asked their designer Yuko Shimizu to come up with a character to appeal to the pre-teen market, she sketched Kitty White. Kitty made her very first appearance on a plastic coin purse.

The cat with nine lives

Hello Kitty has travelled further than her wildest dreams. By 1976, she had made it to the USA. In the USA alone, the brand has expanded into more than 4,000 shops. A Taiwanese airline, Eva Air, adopted Kitty in 2005. She decorates the exterior and interior of an Airbus and the flight attendants' uniforms. In 2009, the Bank of America offered its customers cheques and debit cards bearing the pretty Kitty face.

What's the secret?

Clever marketing means that the Hello Kitty brand can be seen almost everywhere. However, some products are produced in small numbers to boost their desirability. Part of Kitty's appeal is also down to the simplicity of the brand. Because she has a strong image she has been able to move with the times and appear on a wide range of products. This lovable cat spans the age range and has been spotted on wine bottles and even features in Nintendo DS games. Hello Kitty is predictable yet she keeps people guessing – a very clever brand (and Kitty!) indeed.

Hello Kitty flies into New York City — as a giant balloon!

Career highlights

2005 *Hello Kitty: Roller Rescue,* an action adventure game was released on Xbox, GameCube and PlayStation 2

2008 A 'Hello Kitty' themed maternity hospital opened in Taiwan — everything from the nurses' uniforms to the bed sheets sported the famous cat!

2009 iPhone released the highly successful game *Hello Kitty: Parachute Paradise*

The iPhone, Coca-Cola and Aston Martin are all cool brands. Year after year, they are listed in top surveys conducted to find the best brands. What is it about these brands that makes people want them so badly? Are they really that special or is it just all down to clever marketing?

Check out www.astonmartin.com to see some amazing car design and branding!

COOL BRANDS!

Branding

The success of any product is down to many factors, but when it comes to selling things, branding is right up there at the top. The brand of a product or company is its identity – it's what we think when we hear the name. The identity of a brand is bound up in the name, logo, image and marketing of the product or company. When people hear 'iPhone', they already have ideas about that product. Many people will think, 'I'd love one of those'. That proves that Apple, the company that makes the iPhone, has its branding spot on!

Being the best

What makes certain brands cooler than others? In 2010, car manufacturer, Aston Martin beat iPhone to number one on the CoolBrands list in the UK and the BrandZ Top 100 in the USA. In recent years, the iPhone had topped most people's wish lists. So what caused this change in chart position? The answer could lie in the exclusivity of the product. More and more people own an iPhone, making it less exclusive. Meanwhile, Aston Martin cars are so expensive that most people can only dream of owning one.

Face of a brand

For extra selling power, some brands identify people with their product. For example, Harry Potter star Emma Watson has been the face of luxury brand Burberry. In other cases, people such as David and Victoria Beckham, have become brands in their own right.

BRAND NEW START

We are surrounded by brands and it's difficult to imagine a world without the marketing and branding of products. In fact, branding is something that really only took off in the second half of the nineteenth century.

Coca-Cola promoted its brand with clever advertising that lifted the product head and shoulders above the competition.

All change

During the industrial revolution (circa 1750–1900), great changes took place in all aspects of life. This was down to the growth of factories and mass-produced goods. Until then, most people had been used to a limited selection of local produce. After the industrial revolution, they were presented with choice.

Branding begins

Meanwhile, the manufacturers wanted their products to stand out. When they transported their goods from factories, they used a hot iron to mark the factory 'brand' on the barrels and carriages, which is where the term 'branded' originated. Some successful brands that we recognise today were among those great nineteenth century manufacturers, including Kellogg's, Campbell's, Coca-Cola and Levi's. These companies have built up a brand loyalty that has lasted for well over a century.

Coca-Cola is a regular feature at US sporting events — where giant bottles and cans, emblazoned with the iconic logo, advertise this hugely successful brand.

Cool and fizzy

As well as being one of the oldest brands, Coca-Cola is possibly the best-known brand of all time. The drinks company was founded in 1892 in the USA and its famous fizzy beverage is now available in more than 200 countries around the world. Coca-Cola, or 'Coke' as it is known, also has one of the most recognisable logos on the planet!

Lasting logo

The Coca-Cola logo has hardly changed since it was first designed in 1886. The original typeface of Coca-Cola resembled the formal handwriting style of that era. And, it has stood the test of time – appearing on bottles, cans, glasses, billboards and signs through to the present day.

BATTLE OF THE BOOTS

The ugg boot has been around for decades, but in the mid-2000s, it stepped into the limelight. Seen on the feet of supermodels and celebrities, the boot became a fashionista must-have! And so began the boot brand battle…

UGG imitation boots are now sold everywhere, from supermarkets to the high street.

In 1996, Deckers bought the American trademark for the UGG Australia brand.

Looking sheepish

In the past, Australian and New Zealand sheep shearers wrapped sheepskin around their legs to keep warm. They called their crudely-fashioned legwear 'uggs', thought to be from the word 'ugly'. In the 1960s, Australian surfers began wearing uggs and in the 1970s, American surfers followed suit. A seventies surfer from California called Brian Smith started up UGG Holdings Inc., exporting boots from Australia and New Zealand.

Terms and trademarks

In the beginning, 'uggs' was just a generic term for the sheepskin boots made in Australia and New Zealand. This meant that anyone producing the boots in those countries could call them uggs because it was not a trademark. In 1983, the American company, Deckers Outdoor Corporation, bought out UGG Holdings.

Tug of the 'ugg'

Deckers hit the big time in the mid-2000s. This should have been good news for ugg producers everywhere, but then Deckers pulled the plug on anyone else calling their boots 'uggs'. Deckers claimed that UGG was a trademark and only they had the right to use it. Australian and New Zealand manufacturers were furious and so began the battle to keep the ugg name for all. In 2006, the Australian and New Zealand manufacturers finally won the right to use 'ugg' in their own countries.

Style wars

Deckers is determined to fight on in the marketplace. In 2010, it employed famous shoe designer Jimmy Choo to give the boots a style makeover. The limited-edition boots featured animal prints, fringing and studs. The battle for the brand may have ended, but the style wars have only just begun…

By the mid-2000s, celebrities such as Jennifer Lopez (shown here), Kate Moss and Madonna had helped to kick-start a trend for cosy, no-nonsense UGG boots.

LIFESTYLE LABELS

Nike

Nike, as worn by tennis star Rafael Nadal

These days, leisurewear is big business. It doesn't matter if a customer is not a fan of the great outdoors, by buying into brands such as Fat Face, Nike, Quicksilver and Animal, they will look trendy and sporty. How do these clothing companies convince their customers to buy their gear?

The logo

Fat Face promotes itself as the leading designer of clothing and accessories for an active life. The company is all about funky, fashionable clothes that keep people warm on a mountain but look good when they are just hanging out.

The company's logo goes a long way to portray its fresh and cheeky approach to outdoor clothing. With a cartoon-like face and typeface that would not look out of place on a graffiti wall, the logo speaks to fashion-forward kids everywhere!

The brand

Clothing brand Animal aims to win round surfer-types. This company prides itself on 'authentic' surf, snow and board sport clothing. The brand name calls to people who are into action sports – those who have a little bit of 'the animal' in them. At the end of the day, Animal would not have the same appeal if it were called 'Pussycat'!

The slogan

The right slogan is also good for business. Some slogans are so catchy that they have become part of our everyday lives. Worn by sporting greats such as Rafael Nadal and the Williams sisters, Nike will always be remembered for 'Just do it!'.

Fat Face

13

BRAND BUSTERS!

19 BILLION

The number of Lego bricks produced each year!

5th

Biggest country in the world – if the users of Facebook were the population of a country!

3 MILLION

The number of iPads sold worldwide within the first 80 days of its launch in April 2010.

80

The percentage of Nintendo DS owners that are aged between eight and 16 years old.

700 BILLION

The number of minutes spent on Facebook by its users each month.

1.7 BILLION

The servings of Coca-Cola sold each day around the world.

340 MILLION

The number of tweets a day generated on the social networking website Twitter.

124

The number of available languages for Google, the most used search engine in the world.

1 BILLION

The number of Barbie dolls sold since its creation in 1959.

BRAND BECKHAM

Posh and Becks

From the early days of their romance, David and Victoria were always in the news. There were plenty of 'Posh and Becks' tales to tell. In 1999, they had their first child and just a few months later, they were married during a lavish fairytale wedding. Next, they moved into a large stately home, nicknamed 'Beckingham Palace'!

THE STATS

Name: David Robert Joseph Beckham
Born: 2 May 1975
Place of birth: Leytonstone, London, UK
Nationality: British
Job: Footballer, model and UNICEF Ambassador

THE STATS

Name: Victoria Caroline Beckham (nee Adams)
Born: 17 April 1974
Place of birth: Harlow, Essex, UK
Nationality: British
Job: Former Spice Girl, fashion designer, singer-songwriter and model

Style icon

When her music career in the Spice Girls came to an end, Victoria launched a line of sunglasses, a range of denim clothing and a 'his' and 'hers' fragrance line called 'Intimately Beckham'. In 2008, she stunned the fashion world with her 1950s-inspired collection of clothing. The Victoria Beckham Collection has earned her praise from the fashion and celebrity world. Added to this, Victoria gave style advice and fashion tips to Prince William's wife, Catherine, prior to their honeymoon.

The Olympic and football hero

David's talent on the football pitch has earned him hero status and he has the power to sell anything from sports equipment and holidays to aftershave and underwear. Although David was not selected for Great Britain's Olympic football squad, he brought in the 2012 Olympic torch on the ceremony's opening night. From his fame, David has also helped back bids for the 2018 Football World Cup.

Brand it like Beckham

David and Victoria have been in the spotlight for more than a decade. In that time, they have moved on from being colourful celebrities to mega marketing tools. These days, the mighty Brand Beckham is a power to be reckoned with – as well as raising money for charities and boosting bids for the Olympic Games, the brand has the power to sell just about anything from handbags and perfume to football kits.

'The thing that I really care about is making the world more open and connected,' Zuckerberg says.

THE FACEBOOK BILLIONAIRE

By the end of 2011, Facebook had nearly 900 million active users. By October 2012, it had one billion active users – nearly one-sixth of the world's population. Facebook is a social networking phenomenon, but who is the brain behind this famous brand?

Information age genius

Facebook co-founder and president is the youthful American and 'programming prodigy' Mark Zuckerberg. At Harvard, Mark was a typical student who liked a good prank. One weekend in 2003, he set up an internet site called Facemash onto which he uploaded photographs of other Harvard students. Visitors to the site got to vote for the best-looking students! By Monday, the college had shut down the site. Facemash was no more, but it sparked the idea for something big…

Network whirlwind

Fast forward to February 2004 when Zuckerberg launched Facebook. Initially, the site was meant for Harvard students. It was a virtual meeting place where they could catch up with each other's lives. The idea quickly caught on and Zuckerberg expanded the site to other colleges. By summer 2004, Zuckerberg and some fellow students set up their first office in California. There was no turning back. Zuckerberg dropped out of Harvard to concentrate on developing Facebook.

Facing the future

By 2007, Facebook was a global website with more than 150,000 people signing up each day. That same year, Microsoft invested US$240 million (£158 million) in the company, which was worth an estimated US$15 billion (£9.3 billion). In 2012 Facebook bought Instagram, a popular photo-sharing app, for US$1 billion (£629m), despite the fact that the app is free to use! With Facebook translated into more than 100 languages and its popularity growing all over the world, Mark Zuckerberg's dream is definitely on track.

JOHN BENSON

John Benson is one of the founding members of Stocks Taylor Benson, a commercial graphic design company. This team of no-nonsense designers has worked with some of the coolest brands, including Mambo, O'Neill, Quiksilver, Speedo, Thorntons and bmi. Here John tells Radar what makes a cool brand!

What makes a successful brand?

A successful brand is so much more than one product, one logo or one piece of packaging – it's about the complete picture. A winning brand is about the whole company and everything surrounding it. It's about the people working for the company, the design of the products, where the products are sold – it's even down to how the telephone is answered!

How do you create a best-selling brand?

Brands that do well focus on their 'brand values' – the things that set them apart from their competitors. Brands that fail lose sight of their core message and try too hard to appeal to everyone.

What makes an eye-catching logo?

A great logo is not just about making a pretty picture. The logo should be clear and simple. There should be logic to the logo and a really strong reason why it was designed that way.

What is your top tip for creating a winning brand?

My number one tip is to keep things clear. Your branding should be easily understood and it should be obvious at whom it is aimed. If it's a unique product, then this should be made clear. It doesn't matter whether the product is funky and innovative or steeped in tradition – the branding should be straightforward.

What is the story behind the Nike logo?

It was created in 1971 by an American graphic design student called Carolyn Davidson. Philip Knight, the owner of Blue Ribbon Sports, asked her to design a logo for a new sports footwear range he was about to launch, called 'Nike'. Carolyn came up with the now-famous swoosh symbol, which represents a wing of the Greek goddess Nike. So successful was the logo and the footwear that the company changed its name to Nike Inc. in 1978...and the rest is history.

Describe one of your favourite brand campaigns.

The Cadbury's advert in which charity shop clothes dance to Jermaine Stewart's *We Don't Have to Take Our Clothes Off* track is great. It makes people laugh and perfectly conveys the brand slogan 'A glass and a half full of joy'.

What is it about your job that gives you a buzz?

Every time I see something that we've designed I still get a real tingle inside. It could be some packaging in a store, an advert in a newspaper or a logo going by on the side of a lorry...I love it!

LOGO DESIGN

Your logo should be distinctive and relevant. But before you start designing, make sure you understand your market by asking questions and listening to the answers.

You will need:
- paper • pencils • marker pens
- imagination and creativity
- (optional) computer software

1 Collect examples of the kind of graphics that you think a target audience is drawn to.

2 Think about how the name of your brand might lend itself to an image that you can use alongside the word.

3 Write down any ideas that come into your head. Don't spend too long on each idea – try to come up with as many as possible.

4 Take your favourite ideas and fine-tune them. Maybe two of the ideas could be joined together into one great logo?

5 You may want to use computer software to draw the logo neatly and to apply colour. Consider which colours would suit your logo – you might even decide that black and white works best.

Type 'logopalooza 2' into www.youtube.com to see some great logos.

Got it?

Show your logo to friends and note how they react. Are those friends in the target audience? If so, are they attracted to it? If they are, then you've designed a successful logo!

2001 Apple opened its first two retail stores, called Apple Stores, in Virginia and California

2003 The company launched its online music shop, iTunes

2008 Opened the App Store, selling applications such as games and business tools

2011 Apple launches iPad 2, which is faster than the original iPad and features two cameras

THE STATS

Name: Apple Inc.
Born: 1 April 1976
Place of birth: Steve Jobs' bedroom, California, USA

When Apple opened its first Australian store in 2008, crowds queued outside for over 24 hours!

APPLE INC.

The Apple of our 'i'

Computer whiz-kids

Apple Computer Inc. was the brainchild of Steve Jobs and Steve Wozniak. In 1972, the two men met while working for the internet technology company Hewlett-Packard and discovered they both shared an interest in personal computers (PCs). In 1975, they turned their interest into a project and began work on their first PC, the Apple I. In 1976, Ron Wayne, an old work colleague of Jobs', joined them and Apple Computer Inc. was founded.

The early days of Apple Computer were hampered by lack of funds. Amazingly, the team managed to assemble 50 Apple I PCs in just ten days. However, Wayne believed the business was too risky and sold his share of the company after 12 days – a share that would be worth over three billion dollars today!

Byte of the Apple

Jobs and Wozniak were determined to carry on and persevered with the company. Their determination paid off – by the end of the 1970s, Apple was instantly recognisable by its distinctive logo. It also employed a large team of designers and had an efficient production line that created thousands of Apple II computers, one of the first micro PCs to achieve great success.

In 1984, Apple released the Macintosh and in 1998, it launched the iMac, the fastest selling PC in history. The next wave of iMac computers was released in six vibrant colours – a first in the computer world – and Apple's PowerBooks and iBooks seemed ever sleeker and faster with each new model.

Top tech

In the 2000s, Apple switched its focus to mobile electronic devices. In 2001, it released the iPod, a digital music player that became the best-selling portable music player ever. The year 2007 was another turning point in Apple's history as the company changed its name to Apple Inc. and released the revolutionary iPhone and iPod touch. Then, in 2010, Apple launched the iPad, a portable tablet from which users could access the internet, newspapers, ebooks, films and music. In 2012 the iPad mini was launched – a smaller version of the original iPad, with all of the same capabilities.

Big Apple

In 2010, it was announced that Apple had overtaken Microsoft, its rival in the consumer electronics market, to become the top technology company in the world – and one of the most popular 'cool' brands of all time.

BRANDING COMES OF AGE

Brands have moved on since the nineteenth century. Coca-Cola is one of the most valuable brands in the world, but in the twenty-first century there are more brands than ever. Toys R Us, Barbie and Lego are testament to the fact that children become aware of branding from a very early age.

Branding is an everyday part of our culture – whether you are into Barbie or Nintendo, the chances are you have bought a branded product at some point!

Twenty-first century movers

As they grow older, children might switch to sports or technology brands such as Nike or Nintendo. Around the early teenage years, more sophisticated brands begin to take over, such as Apple with its iPhone, iPod and iPad. And that is just the beginning – the brands just keep on coming...

'Google it!'

The Google brand is a web winner. Founded in 1998, the company offers users a free search engine and is the most popular in the world. By 2002, the verb 'to Google' had passed into everyday speech. Today, if anyone has a question about anything, the common response is: 'Google it!'

On average, the Google website has over 2 billion hits every day!

The big screen and beyond

Great brands have something in common – they have built up a strong relationship with the customer. They have done this because they represent excellent products and have moved with the times. They are also so successful because their brand is seen in all the right places. Advertising on billboards, in shops, in magazines, on television and in cinemas, keeps brands in the public eye. Facebook attracted even more attention in 2010, when the story of its creation was told in the film *The Social Network*.

Surfing to success

To succeed in the twenty-first century, the web is where it's at! The big brands target people browsing the internet. Meanwhile, the internet has been the making of many brands. The retailer Amazon and the social networking sites Facebook, MySpace and Twitter have all made their names on the web.

BRAND CHAT

For the coolest brand-speak, check out our Radar guide!

billboard
a large board, usually on the streets, on which advertisements are posted

brand awareness
how much consumers know about a certain brand

brand identity
how others see a brand. Brand identity is created through the brand's logo, marketing and advertising, and the consumers' relationship with the brand

brand loyalty
a person's commitment to buying only one brand or product

brand recognition
how well consumers recognise a brand. For example, the famous McDonald's 'M' alone tells you that you are buying a McDonald's product

consumer
a person that buys and uses a product or service

CoolBrands
the annual list of the UK's coolest brands, people and places. The survey was started in 2001, and the results are published in September each year

exclusivity
describes something that is available only to a limited set of people

logo
some symbols, letters or a graphic representation of a company name or trademark

marketing
the methods, such as advertising, used to tell a consumer about a product

mass-produce
to manufacture goods in large quantities in a factory

motif
a distinctive form or shape often repeated on branded products and associated marketing

slogan
a phrase expressing the aims of a business and repeated in advertising and promotion of the company's products

trademark
a sign that tells the consumer that a product or brand name is owned by the manufacturer

GLOSSARY

brainwashing
using techniques such as advertising to make a person believe something

circa
approximately

conglomerates
corporations that consist of many subsidiary companies or divisions from unrelated industries

debit cards
small plastic cards used as a method of payment. The money is taken from a person's bank account automatically

era
a period of time

fashionista
someone who wears the latest fashions

generic
shared by, typical of or relating to a group of similar things

Harvard
a highly-respected university in Massachusetts, USA

industrial revolution
the period of time from the eighteenth to the nineteenth centuries during which mass-production in factories replaced the man-made production of goods

innovative
using new methods and ideas

manufacturers
companies that produce goods in large numbers

netting (a profit)
earning or making a clear profit after all deductions have been made

packaging
the wrapping and boxes in which a product is sold

phenomenon
something that is impressive and extraordinary

prodigy
a person with exceptional or extraordinary talents

products
things that are made or produced

typeface
a specific style of lettering

UNICEF
a United Nations organisation that protects the rights of children around the world

COOL CULTURE VS GREED?

FOR

Many people adore cool brands and do not mind paying extra for them because they believe branded items are better than 'no-name' ones. They say:

1. Brands say a lot about a person. Cool, branded products signify success and imply that the owner knows what they want and how to get it.
2. People trust the brands they know and see advertised a lot. They feel that Nike trainers (as opposed to lesser-known brands) not only look and feel great, they offer the best in sports technology, too.
3. Some brands go way beyond cool! When a person buys their products they know that the goods are innovative and offer something different from the other 'same-face' companies.
4. People like the exclusivity of luxury brands. They want the things that other people cannot afford – it makes them feel like a million dollars!
5. Buying into a brand can make young people feel accepted and part of the 'club'.

However, other people think that buying into top brands is unnecessary or just plain wrong! They argue that:

AGAINST

1. Cool brands focus on the marketing and branding of a product so much that they sometimes forget about the product itself.
2. It is all a con! People who think that luxury brands are better are just being tricked. For example, handbags that are said to be handmade in Italy are sometimes partly made in China in the same factories where 'no-name' bags are also made.
3. Some brands do well just because large companies are able to fund glitzy advertising campaigns. Advertising is just brainwashing.
4. People do not like the effect of branding on young people. Even children as young as six want the latest mobile phone. This desire to own expensive items creates a 'must-have' mentality and can lead to debt or even crime.
5. Buying into brands can make those who cannot afford cool brands feel left out or inferior.

RIGHT OR WRONG?

Cool or not? Buying into a cool brand gives people a certain social status and can give them a sense of satisfaction that they have bought the very best product available. But if this means that people resort to crime or get into debt to be a part of the brand, the clever marketing is only adding to their own – and society's – problems.

BRAND SPANKING

Get connected

The very best place to find out more about cool brands is on the internet. Most search engines are free, so you can check out your favourite brands and their products without handing over any cash! Disney and Lego also have great free games to play on their websites.

Hit the shops!

Now you can shop for your favourite brands – for free! The games at the Star Doll website feature virtual shops where you can 'buy' fantastic, top brand clothes: **www.stardoll.com**

The Apple store

Visit the Apple website to find out all you need to know about iPad and iPhone and check out the chart news at iTunes: **http://store.apple.com**

Brand awareness

You can keep up with the cool brands just by staying in tune with what is going on around you. Don't forget to look out for branding on the television, on billboards and in magazines.

Reads and Apps

If you want to go deeper into the subject, take a look at these books:

Big Business: Facebook, Nintendo, Apple and *Google* all by Adam Sutherland (Wayland 2011)

Download the *BrandZ100* app from iTunes and discover which brands have made it into the top 100 brands worldwide: **www.itunes.com**

INDEX